Mental Toughness & Discipline Mastery

*Build your Self-Confidence
to Unlock your
Courage and Resilience!*

*(Including a Practical 10-step Workbook
& 15 Powerful Exercises)*

MASTER.TODAY

Roger Reed

Introduction

What is it that distinguishes the most successful people from the rest? The capacity to work hard is, of course, significant. So too is a clear vision of what they are working towards. But there is another, less obvious, attribute that virtually every person who succeeds in any field has in common: mental toughness.

It doesn't matter if you are an entrepreneur or an athlete, a teacher or a student Success does not come easily – to achieve it in any field you must overcome obstacles and deal with problems. Mental toughness is about how you react to adversity, and that is the single most important factor in defining whether you will ultimately succeed or fail.

Mental Toughness is a Superpower

"Our greatest weakness lies in giving up. The most certain way to succeed is always to try just one more time."

- Thomas Edison

Movies, television, and comic books are filled with superheroes, people who have special powers that most people don't have. Unfortunately, you can't learn to become a superhero. But you can learn a superpower that will give you an advantage over most people: mental toughness.

There are lots of names for this power including resilience, tenacity, grit, hardiness, determination, or discipline. It doesn't matter what you call it. What we are discussing here is a state of mind that allows you to see where you want to be and to overcome the barriers that lie between you and that goal. It isn't going to be easy and it will take time but, if you follow the guidance in this book, you will learn how to change your life.

Mental toughness isn't something that you are born with. Studies show that it is something that can be learned,[1] and it is the single most important difference between success and failure. The quote at the beginning of this section comes from Thomas Edison, one of the most prolific and successful inventors the world has ever seen. Edison's inventions were responsible for advances such as electric power, sound recording, and even motion pictures. Without the inventions of Thomas Edison, the world would be a very different place.

But Edison wasn't a genius who had inspirational "Eureka" moments that led to these new ideas. Instead, he worked methodically, testing lots of ideas and accepting that most of these ideas would not become successful inventions. He once claimed that every successful invention came only after testing 10,000 ideas. Edison had the mental toughness to persevere in the face of adversity, knowing that if he continued, he would eventually find success. That persistence changed the world and made Edison a multi-millionaire. You, too, can learn to think like Thomas Edison.

---

[1] *Adapting to Stress: Understanding the Neurobiology of Resilience*, Carlos Osorio, *Behavioral Medicine*, April 2016, King's College, London

This book is about taking action, not just thinking

Prior thought provides the essential underpinning to everything we do, and planning is an important part of taking effective action. It's all too easy to become so mired in thinking and planning that you never actually take action. So, while this book will briefly explain the theories behind mental toughness, it's focused on the things you can actually do to change your life.

That's a scary thought. After all, the one sure way to avoid failure is never to do anything. If you don't try, you can't fail. But if you don't try, you also can't succeed. This book will tell you how to build the mindset and habits that provide mental toughness. That will help you to achieve what you set out to do but mental toughness does not mean that you will never fail. Instead, you will learn to deal with failures in a constructive and positive way and to use these as a step on the path to long-term success.

How to use this book

At the end of this book, you wlll find exercises that are referenced in the text. If you are like most people who read books like this, you will probably be tempted to ignore these.

Don't.

These exercises are a part of building the habits and mindset you need to develop mental toughness. Most of these exercises don't take long to complete, and they will help you make the transition from thinking about this approach to actually applying mental toughness to your life. Remember, this book is not just about changing how you think, it is about changing what you do as well. The exercises are an important element of this approach.

Are you ready to succeed?

How do you know if you need to develop mental toughness? Well, that's fairly simple. Are you satisfied with your life and, in particular, are you happy with the progress you're making towards defined life goals? Mental toughness is not something you only use in your career. It is also about relationships, parenting, and every other aspect of your life. If you can honestly answer *"Yes,"* you don't need this book. Really. You already have mental toughness and perhaps you should think about writing your own book?

For most of us, success is less easy to achieve or even to define. We talk about succeeding a lot in this book but what that word means is personal to you. Perhaps it's about making enough money to support your family, running a successful business, or raising confident, content children. What does success look like to you?

Many people find defining success is difficult. We lack clear goals and the boldness required to take the decisions that can change our lives. We are passive, avoiding stress and problems where we can and accepting the second-best options. It doesn't have to be that way!

This book will teach you:

- How to take control of your life
- How to overcome fear and deal effectively with stress
- How to deal positively with problems and failures
- How to apply the mental toughness approach used by the Royal Marines
- How to make mental toughness a habit

Building mental toughness will take time and effort. Just like building muscles, building mental toughness requires time and repetition but, if you are prepared to follow this step-by-step guide, you can change your life permanently and for the better.

Do you want a superpower? Are you ready to start building the mental toughness that allows you to succeed where others fail? Do you want to change your life?

Then, let's get started!

YOUR FREE GIFT

We would like to give you a gift to thank you for purchasing this book. You can choose from any of our other published titles.

You can get immediate access to any of our books by clicking on the link below and joining our mailing list:

https://campsite.bio/mastertoday

YOU DIDNT COME THIS
FAR TO ONLY COME
THIS FAR

Table of Contents

Chapter 1: What is Mental Toughness and why Does it Matter?

There are a number of definitions of mental toughness. The American Psychological Association defines resilience (the term they use to describe mental toughness) as:

"The process of adapting well in the face of adversity, trauma, tragedy, threats, or significant sources of stress.[2]"

The Journal of Applied Sport Psychology defines mental toughness as:

"Having the natural or developed psychological edge that enables you to generally cope better than your opponents.[3]"

Respected clinical and performance psychologist Dr Jonathan Fader calls mental toughness:

"Being able to push past failures by remaining positive and competitive[4]."

The central theme of these definitions is clear. Mental toughness does not mean that you can avoid stress or

---

[2] *Building your resilience*, multiple contributors, American Psychological Association website, 2012.

[3] *What Is This Thing Called Mental Toughness?*, Jones, Hanton, & Connaughton, Journal of Applied Sport Psychology, 2002

[4] *What is Mental Toughness?*, Dr Jonathan Fader, *Sport Psychology* website.

adversity or that you have to become an emotionless automaton. Instead, it defines how you respond to problems in your life. Do you persevere or do you give up? Learning how to keep going in the face of adversity is the central element of mental toughness and the principal difference between someone who succeeds and someone who fails. Both types of people face adversity and setbacks, but the person who is mentally tough will pick themselves up and keep going until they attain their goal.

We often attribute success to a whole range of abilities. We assume that people succeed in their career because they're smarter, luckier, or because they work harder. We assume that someone makes a good parent because they are more empathetic than other people. We assume that someone be comes a sports star because they have an innate physical ability that allows them to excel at that particular activity. Of course, intelligence and natural ability are important, but one of the most significant (and most often overlooked) aspects of success is mental toughness. Some studies suggest that intelligence accounts for just 25-30% of success. The single biggest contributor to success is mental toughness.

That's good news because, while you can't argue with your genetic inheritance, you can learn mental toughness. But learning mental toughness is actually rather complicated. It involves learning to deal with emotions like anger, disappointment, and frustration in a constructive way. It means learning to focus on the things we want to achieve, not being controlled by our fears. It means thinking honestly about things like:

- Do you cope well with stress and pressure?
- Do you have good self-confidence?
- Are you working towards clear and defined goals?
- Do fear and anxiety stop you from achieving what you want?
- Do you get angry when you fail?

In truth, few of us can give positive answers to all of these questions, and it is tempting to assume that real mental toughness is possessed only by extraordinary people, like the most successful entrepreneurs and top athletes. The truth is that we almost certainly already know ordinary people who are mentally tough.

Think about someone you know who is good at sports. Whatever the sport, ability involves both physical and mental development. You need fitness, agility, and practice to become good at any sport, but you must also have mental toughness. Without that, no matter how proficient you may be physically, you will not consistently succeed.

Do you know someone who is very successful in their career? They probably work hard, but lots of people do that without succeeding. What's the difference? Almost certainly the mental toughness to work towards clear goals and to deal positively with adversity and setbacks. No career, whether you are an employee or an entrepreneur, develops without problems. It's how you respond to those problems that will define whether you ultimately succeed or fail.

Perhaps you know someone who is a great parent? Bringing up children involves dealing effectively with uncertainty and problems. The people who succeed most notably are those who work through those issues without losing their focus or their belief in their ultimate goal.

Think about a police officer, medic, or fire-fighter. All these people deal with high-stress situations, sometimes where lives are at stake. To succeed, all these people must have mental toughness.

Mental toughness isn't something that is unattainable or that is only available to an elite few. It is an approach that can be learned by anyone and applied to every aspect of their lives. It also provides clear benefits.

The benefits of developing mental toughness

Let's take a look at some of the most important benefits of developing mental toughness.

> **Overcoming fear**. Fear is one of the most significant inhibitors of human behavior. That fear can be sensible because it can help us to avoid doing things that may harm us. Fear of failure, fear of the unknown, fear of looking silly, and fear of trying something new all stop us from succeeding. We avoid fear by taking comfort in the familiar and the known. Worst of all, we often don't recognize that fear is involved, telling ourselves that we are being prudent or careful when really, we are allowing our fears to hold us back. Mental toughness helps us to recognize when fear is holding us back and gives us ways to overcome those fears.

Providing clear goals. Overcoming problems is never easy, but we are much more likely to succeed if we see these problems within the overall context of a wider goal. Repeated studies have shown that the most successful people have clear goals that they are working towards. These goals can range from reaching a certain level in sports to setting up a successful business. They focus us on the destination so we are less likely to abandon the journey. Mental toughness helps you to identify and set goals that keep you motivated when you confront problems.

Delaying gratification. Closely linked with long-term goals is the ability to delay gratification. Being human, we want rewards right now. However, grabbing for instant rewards can make us want to give up on something that isn't going to deliver something positive quickly. That's unhelpful because to achieve success in the long term often means hard work and effort now with little immediate prospect of rewards. If we have clear goals, we can learn to delay that impulse in order to work towards gratification in the future.

Dealing with emotions. It is perfectly natural to feel disappointment, frustration, and even anger when you are faced with problems. However, if you direct those emotions at other people, blaming them for your failings, you will never be able to move forward. Mental toughness helps you to understand where your emotions are coming from and how to direct your energies to overcoming problems, not indulging in guilt or blame.

Learning to let go. You tried something new. It failed. That experience hurt. How do you deal with that? If you vow never to put yourself in that position again, then you will never make progress. Instead, you must learn how to accept negative emotions but then move on and let them go. You should learn from the past, but you must not allow past emotions to define how you act now. Mental toughness gives you the techniques you need to let go and move on.

Dealing with self-doubt. Everyone suffers from self-doubt. Everyone, even those who seem totally in control and confident. However, questioning what you are doing is actually healthy, as long as it allows you to learn and grow. Self-doubt is not healthy when it becomes fear that stops you from trying to achieve what you want. Mental toughness allows you to look at what you are doing objectively and openly while rejecting fear.

Dealing with failure. You are going to fail. That is an inevitable part of growing and changing. No one is perfect and everyone makes mistakes. However, mental toughness allows you to see failure as part of a process of learning that will lead to eventual success (remember Thomas Edison!). You should not fear failure, but you must be able to recognize when it's time to stop and spend your time and energy more productively.

Dealing with stress. Achieving almost anything worthwhile involves stress, whether you're trying to be a good parent or to invent some new product. Stress can be harmful if it inhibits holds you back from achieving success, but it can also be motivational if you can learn to see it in the context of overall progress towards important goals. Mental toughness helps you to remain optimistic under stress and to learn to deal with it in positive ways.

Becoming more confident. When you learn to overcome your fears and deal with problems within the context of long-term goals, you are much more likely to have the confidence to keep going instead of giving up. Mental toughness helps you to improve your self-confidence.

Increasing performance. Have you ever tried something new, perhaps a new sport or fitness activity, and then given up? Most of us have, but who knows? Perhaps if we had kept going, we'd now be champions. Mental toughness helps you to perform better in everything you do, to keep going when things get tough.

Mental Toughness Tips from Successful People

It's axiomatic that the most successful people are mentally tough. They wouldn't be successful if they were not. What can we learn from them? Here are some tips for people who have succeeded in their fields.

Forget about luck.

"We don't believe in luck, luck is preparation waiting for an opportunity."

-       Ross Braun, Formula 1 Technical Director

When we look at someone who has succeeded, it's easy to think of them as lucky. We may be tempted to wait for luck to make us successful. The truth is that overnight success is almost always an illusion, and waiting for luck has no part in success. A new product that appears seemingly out of nowhere has almost certainly moved through a long process of development and improvement that we never see. An athlete who attains sudden fame has most likely spent years training and preparing. A successful business is based on years of preparation and, quite possibly, a few failures along the way.

That's really what the quote from Ross Braun is about. You will achieve nothing without preparation. Mental toughness allows you to continue with that preparation even when it does not provide immediate rewards. But, when opportunity presents itself, you will be ready. Others may see it as luck, but you will know better.

Focus on what you can control

"Incredible change happens in your life when you decide to take control of what you do have power over instead of craving control over what you don't."

Steve Maraboli, Author, and Behavioral Scientist

You only have so much time and energy, so it makes sense to concentrate on those things that you can control, and let go of those that you have no ability to change. We are constantly bombarded by information and it's easy to get distracted by things over which we have no control. However, that's not a productive use of your time. Complaining about something is not the same as taking action!

The most successful people focus their time on things they can change They make a clear distinction between what they can change and what they can't. You must learn to do the same and put effort only into those things that you can impact.

Be committed but stay flexible

"The measure of intelligence is the ability to change."

- Albert Einstein

Life has a habit of throwing us the unexpected. It doesn't matter how carefully you plan or anticipate, it's virtually certain that something will appear that you hadn't thought of. How you respond to the unexpected is an important part of mental toughness.

Some people seem to be paralyzed by change. People who are consistently successful are flexible in how they respond to unforeseen developments. You must learn flexibility. That includes accepting that however carefully you may plan, the world is a complex place that may produce surprising developments.

Know yourself

"Don't be confused between what people say you are and who you know you are."

- Oprah Winfrey

Mental toughness requires a deep and true understanding of who you really are and why you do what you do. This understanding involves recognizing and building on your strengths and recognizing and reducing the impact of your weaknesses.

Most of us think that we know ourselves, but that is often true only to a limited extent. We may recognize situations that trigger particular emotions or why we want to receive a particular gratification, but the most consistently successful people clearly understand what drives them. They have personal life goals that matter to them. Deeply understanding yourself is not always comfortable because it may mean acknowledging hidden fears and weaknesses, but it is an essential element of mental toughness.

Learn to deal constructively with disappointment

"If we will be quiet and ready enough, we shall find compensation in every disappointment."

- Henry David Thoreau

No one succeeds at everything, and failure is always a disappointment. Mental toughness means that you respond to disappointment in a different way. If you have worked hard towards achieving something but you have not succeeded, you are not going to feel good about that.

However, you must not allow this disappointment to stop you trying again.

The most successful people feel the disappointment of failure just as acutely, but they use this emotion as an opportunity to analyze and learn what went wrong and, in particular, what they can do to avoid the same failure in future. Developing mental toughness does not mean that you will completely avoid disappointment, but it will mean that you treat this feeling as an opportunity for learning and then you move on.

Achieving real mental toughness means finding a balance between optimism and realism. You need to find that optimism to drive you on to try new things, but this positive view must be tempered with an acceptance that not everything you do is going to work out perfectly. If you are too optimistic, you may fail to anticipate potential problems, and that leaves you open to ever more acute disappointment when they happen. But you must not allow a fear of disappointment to stop you trying.

Embrace uncertainty

"The future is uncertain... but this uncertainty is at the very heart of human creativity."

- Ilya Prigogine, Chemist and Nobel laureate

The future will certainly bring surprises, some welcome, some less so. That's a problem because our plans and aspirations are based on predicting the future but, if it really is uncertain, our plans may have to change. Many people react to this uncertainty by either failing to make long-term plans or giving up when circumstances change.

Mentally tough people view uncertainty as an opportunity. They make plans, but they recognize that these plans may have to change, and they welcome that challenge. Everyone faces uncertainty. Those who learn to accept it and are sufficiently flexible to change according to need will always perform better.

Chapter 2: The Elements of Mental Toughness

The enemies of Mental Toughness

Before we begin to talk about the elements of mental toughness, we first need to discuss several things that are the opposite. These are modes of thought that undermine mental toughness. If you suffer from these ways of thinking, you need to recognize them and to take action to reduce their impact.

It's not fair!

Self-pity is the antithesis of mental toughness. Feeling sorry for yourself because something hasn't worked out is unhelpful. This self-pity leads us to adopt a way of thinking that suggests the problems aren't our fault, that we are helpless in the face of circumstances.

Stop!

You are in control of your life. You make the decisions that lead you towards your goals. If things don't work out, there is simply no point in indulging in self-pity. Of course, you are going to feel disappointed and perhaps even frustrated but at that point, you have a choice. You can wallow in the feeling that the world is against you, that you did your best, but things conspired against you. The unspoken corollary is that there is no point in trying again so that failure becomes an excuse for inaction. Instead, get over failure, learn from it, and avoid making the same mistakes again.

But I'm not good enough...

Self-doubt is a normal human emotion and everyone, even those who seem completely self-assured, suffers from it. This self-doubt can actually be helpful because it causes you to question what you are doing and think about whether there may be better ways. Arrogance is not the same as mental toughness. However, if you allow self-doubt to dominate, it can undermine everything you set out to do.

Self-doubt is often fueled by that voice inside our heads, the one that tells us that we aren't smart, attractive or hard-working enough. Everyone has this internal critic that provides a commentary on what we do whether we want it or not. What many people don't understand is that this inner voice can be trained to become positive and supportive. Instead of telling you that you will never succeed, your inner voice will celebrate success and boost self-confidence. Achieving a positive inner voice is a vital element of building mental toughness.

I can't be bothered

Laziness is another aspect of our personalities that prevents us from succeeding. But the truth is that the less we do, the more we feel sluggish and lethargic. Of course, that doesn't mean that you don't need to take time to relax and refresh. It's about recognizing when you are avoiding something because it just seems like too much effort and about taking steps to make sure our energy remains high.

Self-discipline is an important element in overcoming our natural tendency to want to avoid hard work and stress.

Working towards long-term goals helps us to stay focused and to avoid laziness.

I want this to be perfect...

You might imagine that perfectionism is a part of mental toughness, but in reality, it isn't. Trying to do the best you can in any endeavor is good, but believing that things are only worth doing if you can reach some imagined (and probably unattainable) state of perfection is not. It's a very short step from trying to attain perfection to deciding that it really isn't worth bothering because you won't make it. Mentally tough people are always striving to exceed their own expectations, but they are not obsessed with reaching for unattainable perfection.

I'm scared...

Fear is the greatest single inhibitor of mental toughness. In fact, it's so important that this topic gets a chapter all to itself. For the moment, just be aware that fear is normal and even helpful, but if it is uncontrolled, it can block you from achieving your goals

I'm angry

Feeling emotion is natural and healthy. There are both positive and negative emotions. Joy, hope, and love are all positive. Anger, frustration, and jealousy are negative. Positive emotions make us feel optimistic, strong, and confident. Negative emotions make us feel insecure, uncertain, and full of self-doubt. Part of developing mental toughness is learning to recognize negative emotions, to see clearly where they are coming from, and to ensure that we don't allow these feelings to dominate our thinking.

Many people find themselves stuck in cycles of self-doubt and uncertainty. Mental toughness provides an antidote to both and in this book, we'll introduce you to techniques for ensuring that you learn how to develop positive thinking.

I can't do this because…

Self-limiting beliefs are things we believe about ourselves that constrain what we do. Sometimes, they may be sensible, practical, and avoid wasted effort. You may really want to become a professional basketball player, for example, but if you are not very tall, that probably isn't going to happen no matter how hard you work. Your desire to become a fighter pilot is laudable, but it is probably not going to lead to a career in the Air Force if you are color blind.

However, many self-limiting beliefs are harmful and inaccurate. "I'm too old for a new career", for example, or "I can't find a life partner because I'm unattractive" or "I'm not smart enough to learn a new language". Self-limiting beliefs became a problem when they are based on perceptions of our own weaknesses which are often exaggerated or emphasized. We all have abilities and positive attributes, and we need to be able to balance recognition of our weaknesses with an understanding of our strengths. To become mentally tough, we must learn to recognize these self-limiting beliefs as erroneous and ignore them.

<u>Exercise 1</u>

The seven unhelpful modes of thought described above all inhibit personal growth, and they are hindrances to anyone seeking to improve their lives through developing mental toughness. All of us suffer from at least a few of them. Before you begin your journey of improvement, take five minutes to go to the exercises section at the back of this book, and do the first exercise to determine which affect you. It will only take a moment, but it's important that you complete this exercise before reading any further.

The Elements of Mental Toughness

Now that you recognize the states of mind that undermine mental toughness, it's time to think about just what constitutes being mentally tough. There are four parts to being mentally tough:

- Mastering Emotions
- Dealing with Failure
- Responding to Adversity
- Learning to delay gratification

Each is important, and all are linked. Let's take a look at them in turn.

1: Mastering Emotions

Feeling emotion is part of what makes us human. A common misapprehension is that becoming mentally tough means eliminating emotions. It doesn't, simply because that would be impossible. Instead, we must learn to develop emotional intelligence (sometimes called emotional quotient or EQ). EQ allows us to become not only more aware of our emotions but able to see where they come from and able to prevent emotion from ruling our behavior. This understanding of our emotions helps us avoid making decisions based on fear, anxiety, jealousy or whatever emotion we are feeling. That means better decisions but developing EQ also gives us a better insight into other people's emotions, something that is essential if we are to from effective personal and working relationships.

We often assume that intelligence (intelligence quotient, or IQ) is the most important attribute in deciding whether we succeed or fail. However, most studies conclude that EQ is actually a better predictor of success than IQ. IQ leads to academic brilliance, but EQ prepares you for dealing with people. If you can't form effective relationships then, no matter how brilliant you are, you are unlikely to succeed. In a study by the Center for Creative Leadership looking at the causes of career failure, up to 75% were due to some form of problems in working with other people, often due to a failure to fully understand what others want and need in a working relationship.

There are four main elements to EQ:

> **Self-awareness.** You must be able to recognize your own emotions and understand where they come from. Are you angry because you didn't get that promotion or feeling jealous towards the colleague who did? When you can clearly see where negative emotions come from, it's much easier to diminish their impact. Developing strong EQ means reconnecting with your emotions and becoming comfortable with them. It's much easier to stay motivated and to be disciplined when your

behavior isn't being dictated by uncontrolled behavior.

Exercise 2: Assessing your emotions and your awareness of them

Empathy. The word empathy is often used as a synonym for "niceness" or "sympathetic," but that isn't what it means at all. Being empathetic means being able to understand other people's feelings, to put yourself in their shoes. It means being able to understand what other people are feeling and having some idea of why they are feeling that way. Why does that matter? First of all, it allows us to better understand why people act as they do. If your boss is angry, you may assume that your performance is the problem. If you know that your boss is going through personal issues, you may regard their anger quite differently and respond appropriately. Without empathy, you are going to find understanding personal and work relationships much more difficult.

Exercise 3: Empathy

Self-management. Mastering emotions is not about stifling or ignoring what we feel. Trying to disassociate from our feelings or pretend that they don't exist is neither helpful nor effective. That doesn't make us mentally tough, it actually makes us more prone to depression and doubt. Instead, you must learn to manage your emotions by recognizing them, understanding where they come from and learning how to limit their effect on your behavior. Taking action while you are angry, frightened, or anxious is rarely beneficial. Learn to assess your own emotions (and those of others) before making important decisions.

Managing relationships. Whether it's in our personal lives or at work, learning to effectively manage relationships is an essential part of building EQ. Building effective and satisfying relationships requires both empathy and self-awareness. It involves listening to other people (and that means both hearing what they say and becoming aware of nonverbal communication). It means being aware of the effect your verbal and nonverbal communication has on others. No two people are ever going to have precisely the same needs, ambitions, and aspirations so some form of conflict is inevitable. However, by managing relationships effectively you can convert conflict from a source of problems into a way of growing trust.

2: Dealing with Failure

You are going to fail. <u>No one, no matter how talented and hard-working they are,</u> goes through their life without experiencing failure. The more you are willing to take chances and open yourself to new experiences and new opportunities, the more likely you are to fail. But you cannot succeed if you are not willing to take risks. The only way to be certain that you will never fail is never to try to succeed.

Accepting that fact is an important part of learning to deal with failure. If your approach is that you are going to avoid failure completely, the only way to do that is to do nothing. If your approach is that you are going to do your best to succeed but you recognize that won't always happen, that is a much healthier attitude and one that contributes to mental toughness.

Failures are never going to be fun, but that's OK. You will feel bad when you fail, but a 2017 study published in the *Journal of Behavioral Decision-Making* notes that feeling bad about failure can actually motivate you if you look not at the failure itself but at the emotions it provokes in you. Telling yourself you don't care when you fail probably isn't true, and it is not an effective way of dealing with failure. Using alcohol, drugs, or food to blunt your feelings of failure or trying to find another person or circumstance to blame are also not effective responses to failure. You must learn to take something positive from failure – learning. The great thing about failure is that it teaches you how to avoid the same problem in future in the most graphic way. How many people do you know who repeat the same behavior time after time although it has led to failure every time in the past? Perhaps it's an attempt to lose weight, adopt a healthy lifestyle, or change the way that they approach relationships. Yet you are certain that the new approach is doomed to failure in just the same way as previous attempts.

They say that the definition of insanity is doing the same thing over and over, expecting different results. Failing over and over for the same reasons is just the same. Mental toughness means learning to deal with failure in a constructive way. Learn to accept an occasional lack of success as an inevitable result of being bold enough to try something different. Take responsibility but don't take it personally. A lack of success does not mean that <u>you</u> are a failure. You are never going to love frustration, but if you can see it as a valuable learning opportunity and a step on the road to eventual success, then you're well on the way to mental toughness.

Failure is not a kind of global exam result deciding whether you succeed or not. It's just life's way of providing constructive feedback on what you need to change. Take that feedback, learn from it, and move on.

<u>Exercise 4: Dealing with failure</u>

3: Responding to Adversity

Sometimes, life is easy. You coast along with no major issues and achieve what you want with little effort. However, all too often, life isn't like that at all. You spend all your time fighting against problems and obstacles and sometimes it seems like you are barely making any progress. That's adversity, and how you respond to it is an important element of whether you succeed or fail.

Here are four proven techniques for dealing with adversity.

> **Be prepared.** Almost two hundred years ago, British Prime Minister Benjamin Disraeli said *"I am prepared for the worst, but hope for the best."* That approach is just as valuable now as it was then. Optimism is an important element of mental toughness. However, if you can anticipate problems and plan how to respond, you are more

likely to be able to take purposeful, effective action.

Remember what you have achieved. You have faced adversity before in your life and you have succeeded. That knowledge gives you the strength and focus to deal with new problems, and what you learned from past adversity can be applied again. Just like failure, adversity is a way of learning and growing. See it that way and you will find it easier to deal with.

Adversity may provide opportunity. Difficult situations may provide an opportunity for a change of direction or emphasis. In *Think and Grow Rich*, author Napoleon Hill notes that *"Every adversity has the seed of an equivalent or greater benefit."* Think of the COVID 19 pandemic. That event has caused massive and unforeseen problems for companies and individuals around the world. However, a few achieved notable success by embracing the opportunity to change the focus of what they did to better meet the needs of a world in lockdown.

Take control. Unforeseen things happen which you cannot control. You do have control over how you respond. When something unexpected happens, then of course you will want to take the time to reflect, but ultimately your aim should be to take action. You cannot change anything by thinking or planning. Only action leads to change, and if you want to deal with adversity, you must be prepared to act.

Just like dealing with failure, an important part of being prepared for adversity is recognizing that you will likely encounter it in one form or another. Then, it won't come as a complete surprise and you can react more effectively.

4: Learning to delay gratification

Many studies confirm that we are more likely to succeed if we practice self-control and especially if we can learn to delay gratification. What does that mean? It means rejecting the opportunity to do something we enjoy right now in order to achieve something even more important in the future. You may enjoy going for an after-work drink with friends though you could use that time to work on the novel you keep talking about. You make a conscious decision to reject doing something you that will give immediate pleasure (going for a drink) and instead you focus on something that will bring a greater benefit later (having a novel published).

You will note that delaying gratification involves a conscious decision on your part. You are in control of whether you go for the lesser pleasure now or the greater benefit later. However, it is notable that the ability to delay gratification is an important part of mental toughness and a feature of the most successful people. In part, delaying gratification is about learning impulse control. You're on a diet, you're hungry, and you pass a cake shop with delicious pastries in the window. Your impulse is to rush in and buy one. Delaying gratification means that you don't because you want your diet to succeed.

The good news is that, just like every other part of becoming mentally tough, you can learn to delay gratification. Every time you give in to an impulse, you are reinforcing notions in your brain that associate pleasure with minimal effort. That association becomes a habit, and it's not a helpful one. Conversely, when we make the effort not to give in to impulse, we are learning to delay gratification and to make an association between self-restraint, discipline and reward. If you can learn to delay gratification you will be sharing a state of mind with the most successful people.

Learning to think this way is not easy. Every day, we are bombarded with messages designed to persuade us to give in to impulses. We must learn to reject those in favor of following our long-term goals.

Chapter 3: Overcoming Your Fears

Fear is useful. It stops us doing things that may harm us, it ensures that we remain alert, and it can even prompt us to take action. However, fear can also be a barrier to action if we allow it to dominate our thinking and seek only what feels like the least risky option, instead of logically weighing the alternatives. Fear can intrude in every part of our lives from our career to our relationships.

Part of dealing with fear is learning to recognize it. Feeling fear is something that affects everyone, but it's actually harder to identify than you might think. If we encounter a dangerous animal in the wild or find ourselves in a precarious position high above the ground, the fear we feel is immediate and unmistakable. However, that kind of simple fear is (hopefully!) rare in our working lives and relationships. Instead, we suffer from complex fears that can be more difficult to define and explain.

To develop mental toughness, you must learn to recognize and overcome fear. Fortunately, there are a number of proven techniques you can use to do this.

Name that Fear

One of the best techniques for dealing with fear is called *"naming your fear."* Just like almost anything else that affects our behavior, really understanding what a particular fear is about is a good way to diminish its subconscious effect. That's actually more complicated than it sounds when you're dealing with complex fears. For example, you may say that you are afraid to try something new at work because if it doesn't work out, you could lose your job. That fear might sound simple and straightforward but, there is more to fear than you might think.

The fear of losing your job is a large, poorly defined fear but it is underpinned by lots of other, more specific, fears. "If I lose my job, I'm afraid that I won't be able to provide for my family." "If I lose my job, I'm afraid I will lose the respect of my partner." "If I try something new and it fails, I am afraid that I will look stupid to my colleagues." These are just examples, but when you drill down into any complex fear, it is usually underpinned by lots of more specific concerns. Naming your fear effectively means thinking these issues through until you understand what is really holding you back.

If there is something that you keep putting off, or a task or enterprise that you just can't seem to get started on, it is very possible that fear may be involved.

<u>Exercise 5: Naming your fear</u>

What's the worst that can happen?

People have been thinking about how to deal with fear for a very long time. Seneca the Younger was a Roman philosopher and statesman and around 2,000 years ago he founded a new school of thought, stoicism. This philosophy was based on the premise that overcoming emotions including fear was an essential pre-requisite for living an effective and satisfying life.

Seneca was the first to introduce an exercise intended specifically to reduce fear "*premeditatio malorum*" (the premeditation of evil). In simple terms, this approach involves visualizing, in great detail, the worst-case scenarios for any planned course of action. In the modern business world, Seneca's approach has been re-imagined as "pre-mortem," and it is a recognized and effective management strategy used when planning new enterprises.

A number of large corporations regularly use the pre-mortem technique. NASA, for example, uses pre-mortem workshops to identify the potential problems that may be associated with a new project. Imagining the worst that can happen is actually a powerful planning tool. It is sometimes called *"prospective hindsight,"* meaning that if you can imagine in detail the worst that can happen, you can also think about what may have led to that situation. You can then make plans to ensure that this does not happen.

However, pre-mortem is also a great way of reducing fears. Those worst-case scenarios are a prime cause of fear. If you face up to them and actually think about them in detail, that will lessen those fears. Individuals can use the pre-mortem technique too.

<u>Exercise 6: What's the worst that can happen?</u>

Live for Today

Thinking about the worst that may happen in the future can help in reducing fear. But you don't live in the future. You live here in the present and you must also learn to focus your energy, attention and time on what you're doing right now.

One of the first globally popular self-help books was *How to Stop Worrying and Start Living* by American writer and lecturer Dale Carnegie. First published in 1948, the central thesis of the book is that spending time worrying about the future is largely a waste of time. If instead you can give 100% of your effort to what you do every day, the future will take care of itself. Learning to focus on the present is a powerful approach that is just as relevant now as it was back in 1948.

Thinking about the future and considering what you can do to mitigate potential problems is sensible. Simply worrying about the future in an unstructured way which is completely helpful. You must learn to balance planning for the future with a focus on the present, being 100% committed to what you are doing now. Or, as Dale Carnegie said, *"Just live each day until bedtime."*

Smart Quitting

"Winners don't quit!" is a mantra you will frequently hear repeated in self-help books and elsewhere. There is a degree of truth in it. After all, you need the persistence and tenacity to keep going in the face of adversity. But never giving up is also a fallacy. One of the defining characteristics of successful people is that they know when to quit, and they do it at the right time and for the right reasons. Sometimes, quitting isn't just the most effective approach. It's the only way to make real progress.

However, just as fear can stop you from starting something, it can also make you keep going long after it's evident that your idea isn't going to work. We have already discussed how a willingness to try new things is at the heart of positive change. Sometimes, this inevitably means failure to meet your objectives. How can you ensure that you don't waste time and effort by persisting with an unproductive idea for too long?

Before you even start working on your new idea, you must have clear objectives and review points. Some new ideas will work. Some won't. You need to overcome your fears in order to kill ideas that won't deliver. Building in review points at the beginning (times when you will sit down and consider whether you are achieving what you set out to do) will make you take an objective look at progress.

Being objective is vital here. The fear of giving up is just as powerful as the fear of failing. In fact, not giving something up can simply be a way of delaying recognition that it is going to fail. It can mean fooling yourself that you are dealing with something when you are not or avoiding the possibility of looking foolish. You only have so much time and energy, and you need to spend them where they are most productive. You need to review what you are doing and the progress you have made and decide whether the project is worth continuing. Deciding to quit is not easy. You have an emotional connection to the new idea, and you want it to succeed. Giving up feels like failure. However, quitting can also bring important learning opportunities. If you try something and it doesn't work, consider why and what you have learned from the experience.

Winners do quit. In fact, studies show that the most successful individuals quit more than most. But they quit for the right reasons, and they learn from that experience.

Don't let fear trap you into continuing with something long after it's obvious it won't achieve what you want.

Dealing with problems

A major inhibitor of positive change is a fear of problems, real or perceived. You'd like to get fitter, but you probably won't be able to find the time. You'd like to get more involved in IT at work, but you just don't know enough about computers.

Just like dealing with fear itself, the impact of problems can be diminished by facing them and trying to understand them. Take the first example above. You want to improve your fitness, but you think that finding the time may be a problem. There are a couple of things to think about here. The first is practical. Just what are you trying to achieve and how much time will it take each week? Write out a schedule and see how that fits into your life. If it seems too much, why not try spending a little less time on it. You can still improve your fitness by doing less exercise. Can you swap taking the car to work for walking or parking the car further away and walking part of the way? Focus on the goal – getting fitter – and the benefits that will bring. You can find the time to fit that in, no matter how busy you are.

However, not all problems are as practical as how to fit exercise into a busy schedule, and not all can be solved so simply. Often, our perception of problems is nothing more than hidden fear. You want to get fitter, but inside, you are afraid that you won't be able to do it. You rationalize by saying that you don't have time, but really the problem is your fear of failure. Failing to recognize the importance of emotions such as fear is a very common situation, and it is why looking in detail at problems can help not just to resolve them, but to reveal the underlying feelings that may lie behind them.

Recognizing which are which is important. Real, practical problems are susceptible to real, practical solutions. Perceived problems that are a mask for fear can only be addressed by facing them and using the techniques previously described for dealing with fear. To be certain what you are facing, you need self-awareness and an understanding of your emotions. When you are dealing with perceived problems, simply looking at them in detail can make them disappear.

There are several recognized techniques for examining practical problems. One of the most effective and popular is "reframing." This technique means not immediately looking for a solution to the problem but looking for different ways to see the problem. Looking at the problem in a different way can lead to being able to identify more obvious solutions. For example, if we go back to the desire to get fitter, the problem is that you don't have time to go to the gym several times a week. If you reframe the problem instead as "how can I get fitter?" instead of "how can I find time to go to the gym?" a solution is easier to find. Instead of seeking time to go to the gym, you can consider how to incorporate more exercise in your daily life, by walking rather than using the car, for example. Simply by looking at the problem in a different way, reframing, a solution becomes obvious.

Renowned scientist Albert Einstein summed this up. He was asked how he approached solving problems and his answer was:

"If I had an hour to solve a problem, I'd spend 55 minutes thinking about the problem and five minutes thinking about solutions."

Spending time looking at problems in order to see then differently is an effective way to find solutions. Sometimes, simply looking at a problem in a different way can make it disappear completely. Learning to deal confidently with problems is an important part of mental toughness and a great way to reduce fear.

Chapter 4: The Precise Application of Will: Learn to Think like A Royal Marine

When we think of tough people, many of us think of special forces soldiers. However, we generally think in terms of physical toughness and the ability to endure extreme events. For special forces soldiers across the world, their training and preparation emphasize mental toughness just as much as physical preparedness. What can we learn from their training that can be applied to developing mental toughness in everyday life?

The Royal Marines

The Royal Marines were first formed in 1664 to serve as soldiers on board the warships of the Royal Navy. During World War II, the first Royal Marine Commando units were formed. These special services troops conducted raids on occupied Europe. In 1950, the Royal Marines became completely commando-focused and the green-beret - wearing troops are now regarded as some of the finest special service soldiers in the world.

Such troops must learn to fight in circumstances where they are far from friendly troops and often outnumbered and outgunned. Training courses at the Royal Marine Commando Training Centre at Lympstone in East Devon involve extreme physical challenges, as you might expect. These training courses are also designed to build the mental toughness required to succeed in the most difficult and challenging battlefield circumstances. Part of this training involves teaching recruits to deal with fear. Reducing fear is often done by placing trainees in frightening situations such as heights or enclosed spaces. Being exposed to fear repeatedly reduces the effect impact of that fear, as we have already discussed in the preceding chapter. Royal Marines are not fearless, they learn to deal with fear by facing it, recognizing it, and by planning for the worst possible outcome.

In addition, Royal Marine training emphasizes four mental qualities unity, adaptability, humility, and fortitude[5]. All four are important elements of mental toughness.

Unity

Unselfishness is regarded as a prime Royal Marine characteristic, and during training, all recruits are expected to constantly help and support their fellow Royal Marines. A selfless devotion to the success of the mission and the survival of the unit over consideration for self is paramount. The worst condemnation a Royal Marine can receive during training is to be identified as a selfish *"Jack,"* as in, *"I'm all right, Jack."* *"Jacks"* rarely complete their training because they are unable to subsume their own needs and desires to the collective good of the group.

Are you a *"Jack"*?

Many of us are. Some people mistakenly see selfishness and a single-minded pursuit of self-interest as being a

---

[5] *The Ethos of the Royal Marines: The Precise Application of Will*, Dr Anthony King, Department of Sociology, University of Exeter, 2004

positive and even admirable approach to life. Some regards these attributes as demonstrating mental toughness. The opposite is true. Selfishness and jealousy are driven by fear and insecurity. Selfish people seem to feel that there is only a certain amount of success available, and if someone else succeeds, that leaves less for them. Of course, that's a fallacy. To be truly selfless, to give help and support where it is needed, is a sign of complete confidence and mental assurance.

Precisely the same thing applies to successful athletes. In his book *The Way of The Champion*, sports psychologist Jerry Lynch notes that the members of the highest performing teams regularly display *"unconditional willingness to put the team or group before any of his/her individual or self needs.*[6]*"* Real winners don't look at every situation by asking *"What's in it for me?"* They consider how to benefit the whole team. and the greatest champions come from the teams that work most effectively together.

But you don't belong to a special forces unit or a high-performing sports team, so how do their abilities apply to your day-to-day life? Very few activities that you do, whether they involve your career, relationships or even hobbies, will be done alone. You, too, work as part of a team and if the team performs well, you benefit. Think of it in like a financial investment. By putting effort into supporting the team rather than just looking out for

---

[6] *The Way of the Champion: Lessons from Sun Tzu's the Art of War and Other Tao Wisdom for Sports & Life*, Jerry Lynch Ph.D., Tuttle Publishing, 2006.

yourself, you are helping the team to succeed. When the team is successful, you, too, will succeed, far more than you could on your own.

A number of studies confirm that workplace loneliness is a growing problem. A 2017 study by California State University and the Wharton School of Business[7] surveyed several hundred workers and found that feelings of loneliness in the workplace were a prime cause of emotional withdrawal and poor performance at work. Similar studies in other countries have found the same thing. Workers who feel isolated and emotionally distanced perform worse. By building supportive relationships, you can decrease feelings of isolation in other members of the team and help boost overall performance.

Like many of the best investments, you may not see an immediate return. In the long term, becoming a team player will bring greater returns. Remember how we talked about the importance of delaying gratification? The more you give, the more you will ultimately receive. The Royal Marine ethos of unity requires dedication to the team but, in return, it gives increased potential for success and greater mental toughness.

Don't be a *"Jack."* Work on developing selflessness. Become an enabler, combining compassion with the confidence to speak out when necessary. Shift your focus from yourself to the people around you and the team to

---

[7] *Work Loneliness and Employee Performance*, Ozcelik, H. and Barsade, S., California Sacramento University, College of Business Administration, 2018.

which you belong, whether that is a family or a group of friends or colleagues.

Adaptability

The future is uncertain, no matter how carefully we may plan. Dealing effectively with the unexpected is even more important for organizations like the Royal Marines. It is unsurprising that the second element of the Royal Marine ethos is adaptability, the ability to deal effectively with the unexpected.

However, adaptability is important in other areas of life too. New technology, social change, and unforeseen developments like the COVID 19 pandemic mean that we cannot say with complete confidence just what the future will look like. Within each life there are significant changes, too. These include changes in career and relationships, moving to different areas, and longer-term changes like becoming a parent and retiring. All we can be truly certain about is that the future is uncertain.

The Greek philosopher Heraclitus summed it up nicely more than two thousand years ago:

"No person ever steps in the same river twice, for it's not the same river, and it's not the same person."

For many people, uncertainty is frightening, and the prospect of change something to be dreaded. The most successful people, those who are mentally tough, don't feel that way. They embrace change and uncertainty because they know that both bring opportunity. The key to maintaining your mental wellbeing in the face of change is adaptability. What do we mean by that? The American

Psychological Association (APA) provides a useful definition of adaptability as *"the capacity to make appropriate responses to changed or changing situations; the ability to modify or adjust one's behavior in meeting different circumstances or different people.[8]"*

How can you develop an adaptable mindset? A large part of adaptability is how you view and react to failures and problems. If you learn how to respond effectively to failure and how to overcome problems, you will be more confident in facing uncertainty. Even better, if you view failure as an opportunity to learn, you will come to see it as just another step on the road to success. Just as important is the ability to remain optimistic, to see change and challenge as temporary and capable of being changed to your advantage.

Seeing opportunity in change and having the mental toughness to remain optimistic are the most important elements of dealing with uncertainty. For his book *Crucibles of Leadership*, Professor Robert J Thomas of Georgetown University interviewed a number of the highest-performing business and public sector leaders. Some of the most notable shared characteristics he found were *"adaptive capabilities,"* the ability to see uncertainty within a positive context and the mental toughness to deal with change. Professor Thomas also found that being able to deal effectively with uncertainty increased mental toughness.

---

[8] *APA dictionary of psychology* (2nd ed.). VandenBos, G. R. (Ed.). (2015), American Psychological Association.

Adaptability is one of the keys to dealing with an ever-changing world. You can't control the future you face, but you can change your mindset to deal more effectively with whatever it may bring. The Royal Marines' emphasis on adaptability is as important for the rest of us as it is for special service soldiers.

Humility

Self-confidence is an important element of mental toughness. You must learn to trust your own judgement and follow your instincts. However, if self-confidence tips over into arrogance, it actually becomes unhelpful. Arrogance implies an acceptance that things are as good as they can be, that you have reached a point where you have learned all you can. That leads to a lack of progress. No matter how successful you become, you must always remain open to learning and improvement, You must be self-critical, to look for new practices and approaches that may make you even more effective.

Being an effective team member fosters *esprit de corps*, pride and loyalty to that group. That must not be allowed to lead to arrogance, a feeling that your team is better than any other. Within the Royal Marines, training never suggests that one unit is better than any other. There is emphasis on the importance of operating with other units, each bringing its own strengths and abilities to any situation.

A number of studies have shown that humility is associated with all sorts of benefits including:

- A clearer sense of life goals
- Increased productivity and harmony in the workplace
- Better relationships
- Longer-lasting marriages
- Improved health.

Humility is also directly connected to creating stronger communities. Humility is the antidote to the ego, the part of our mind that is concerned solely with ourselves. The ego is powerful and, left unchecked, it can dominate our thinking and make us arrogant and selfish.

However, humility within the context of mental toughness involves a difficult balancing act. You need the self-confidence to believe that you can achieve anything you set out to do. Self-confidence must be tempered with the recognition that you may occasionally fail and that there is always space for learning and improvement. If you want to get better at everything you do, you must first learn humility. Or, in the words of Greek philosopher Socrates:

"True knowledge exists in knowing that you know nothing."

Many people confuse humility with weakness and uncertainty. Instead, it is the opposite. It is accepting that no person will ever be perfect or truly complete, no one will ever understand everything. Mental toughness means looking at everything you achieve in that context, of recognizing that no matter how much experience you have or how much you know, there is always more to learn. It means being willing to ask for help when you need it and to learn from what others are doing. It means really listening to other people, seeking honest feedback, and being grateful for what you have.

Life is a journey, and mental toughness helps you to make progress in the direction you choose. If mental toughness is allowed to become arrogance, it can become a barrier. Arrogance will make you believe you have progressed as far as you can. Confidence tempered with humility will ensure that you continue to make progress towards your goals.

<u>Exercise 7: Take a humility test</u>

<u>Exercise 8: What did you learn today?</u>

Fortitude

The fourth pillar of the Royal Marine ethos is fortitude, the ability to keep going in the face of adversity. Much of their training is about developing fortitude though facing physical and mental challenges. They are expected to perform when they are fatigued, faced by seemingly overwhelming odds and in the face of extreme danger. They must do this time after time. Fortitude is not about a single exceptional performance; it is about consistently performing to your best, whatever the situation.

Within the context of mental toughness, we are talking primarily about mental rather than physical fortitude. That willingness to persevere should not be confused with a stubborn insistence on keeping going in the same direction whatever happens. We have already discussed how sometimes, recognizing failure and moving on to something more productive is the most effective response. Mental fortitude means continuing to work towards your goals, whatever happens.

One of the most important elements of mental fortitude is optimism. You must not allow yourself to dwell on pessimistic thoughts and self-doubt. There will be times when things happen that you wish hadn't or when you make decisions that are later revealed to be mistakes. If you fixate on those, you will not be able to take effective action. Instead, you must be able to learn and to move on, leaving these mistakes behind. Your attitude defines how you perform. You must constantly deal with your emotions and look for positive factors even in failure and adversity.

The most successful people, those who have had the greatest impact on the world, are not necessarily the most intelligent, the strongest or the most educated. They are almost always people who display extreme fortitude in the face of adversity. Take the example of a man born in extreme poverty who had two failed businesses and had stood for election in local and national legislature and had been defeated eight times. The same man endured a nervous breakdown following the sudden death of his childhood sweetheart. That man had faced the kind of adversity that most of us will never know. His name was Abraham Lincoln and at the age of 51 he became the 16th President of the United States.

Lincoln helped define the history of the 19th century and became one of the most famous world leaders. He was aided by passion, self-belief, and intelligence, but most of all, his success was due to fortitude in overcoming adversity.

To have the mental toughness of a Royal Marine, you must have unity, adaptability, and humility. Even if you have all of these attributes, without the fortitude to keep going when you encounter problems, you will never achieve what you set out to do.

Chapter 5: Developing Mental Toughness

Up to this point, this book has been about gaining an understanding of what mental toughness is and why it is important. Now it's time to move on from theory to look at how you can apply this knowledge to your life. It's time to stop thinking about mental toughness and to start doing it. Before we start, ask yourself a fundamental question:

Do you want to grow?

Developing mental toughness will not be easy. It will take time and effort. Hopefully you now understand the benefits mental toughness will bring, but is your desire to grow and improve strong enough?

No one else can develop mental toughness for you. You must be able to find the mental resources to continue. Are you sufficiently motivated to do that?

If you are not certain, we will take a look at one of the pillars of mental toughness: setting goals. Having clear goals provides the motivation you need to continue and allows you to assess progress.

Setting Goals

The most successful people don't just drift through life, stumbling over opportunity through happenstance. Instead, they have clear and defined goals they work towards. All their time and effort are used working towards those goals. This dedication is one of the single most important differences between people who succeed and people who fail.

Take the example of one successful entrepreneur. As a child, he was given a die-cast toy, a Porsche 911. He loved the toy car so much that he decided that he wanted to own a real one before he was thirty-five. When he left school, he kept the toy and placed it on his desk where he could see it. It became his prime motivation. When he was tired, discouraged, or just losing focus, glancing at this shiny model car reminded him of what he was working towards and provided reinvigoration.

He made enough money that he was able to buy a beautiful silver Porsche 911 a few months before his 35th birthday. He is in his late 60s now and owns a string of successful businesses. He still owns that 911 because it reminds him of the need for focus to achieve what you want. Without having that car as a goal, he freely admits that he would never have found the focus to attain success.

Now, striving to own a sports car may not seem like a particularly admirable goal (and he never told anyone about his desire to own a Porsche at the time). Goals are personal, and provided they keep you focused, then that's a positive thing. Even seemingly selfish goals can also benefit other people. That entrepreneur was motivated by his desire to own a Porsche. But on the way to attaining that goal, he built several businesses that provided employment to a number of people and became sufficiently wealthy that he now regularly gives to charity. His goal was entirely selfish, but the focus it brought provided positive things along the way.

Your goal doesn't have to be a fancy car or even making lots of money. However, if you are going to succeed, you do need one or more clear, personal goals.

Goals aren't just vague aspirations. To be effective, goals must be SMART. This acronym is widely used in the business world and it stands for:

- **Specific** (simple, sensible, significant)

- **Measurable** (meaningful, motivating)

- **Achievable** (agreed, attainable)

- **Relevant** (reasonable, realistic and resourced, results-based)

- **Timed** (having a clear finish date)

Let's look at these requirements:

> **Specific** is fairly obvious. You need to be able to say when you have achieved a goal. "I want to be happy" is understandable as a goal, for example, but it is too vague. There will never come a point in your life where after which you will always be happy. You cannot say when you have attained that goal. You need to think about what it is that will make you happy and drill deeper for specific goals. Perhaps being happy means being free from money worries. That's clearer, but better still is a specific goal like, "I will be free from all debt."

> **Measurable** is also simple. Again, a vague goal won't work. For example, you can't measure concepts like "happiness" or "worry." "I will be

free from all debt" is much better because you can clearly measure when you have achieved that goal.

Achievable means just what it says. Your goals are the things that will motivate you and keep you focused. But, if they are not achievable, they will simply lead to discouragement and loss of focus. So, be realistic here. Can you really achieve what you set as a goal? Can you see a clear and defined path that uses the skills and experience you have (or that you can attain) to reach your goal? If not, it's probably not achievable.

Relevant refers to whether the goal really matters to you. Is it something you really want and that you are willing to commit time and effort to achieving? Will achieving that goal motivate you?

Timed means setting an end-date for achieving the goal. This deadline helps you to remain focused and gives you something to work towards. So, "I will be debt free within three years" is an even better goal.

To be most effective, goals should always be positive. "I will take a training course to make myself more effective at work" is a positive goal. "I want to mess-up less" is not. Positive goals support a positive mindset and, as we have already discussed, positive thinking is an important part of developing mental toughness. Goals are also important because they help you to avoid relying on external validation. Many of us judge how well we are doing by listening to the opinions of others. Other people's opinions are reliable because others do not always have our best interests in mind. Personal goals give you an objective way of judging the progress you are making and make it easier to ignore or disregard unhelpful advice and opinions.

You must also take ownership of your goals. Remember, these objectives are not intended to impress other people. They must be goals that truly matter to you. If you adopt a goal because you feel you ought to, you will never put the required effort into achieving it. Take losing weight, for example. Many of us probably feel that we could do to lose a few pounds, but is that goal really important enough to us to be a goal? Many of us have started a diet or tried to adopt healthy eating habits but failed to keep it up. We generally ascribe these failings to a lack of willpower or self-discipline, but the real cause is often that we are not fully committed to a particular goal. If not, then that goal is just not going to provide the motivation we need.

Your goals must really matter to you. Whether that means saving the world or owning a shiny sports car depends on your interests. Be absolutely and completely honest with yourself when setting personal goals.

Having goals will not create mental toughness. But these goals will help you make and sustain the effort needed to achieve mental toughness. Without goals, you are adrift and lost. With goals, you have a road map for the journey ahead and a strong motivation to reach your destination.

Exercise 9: Setting Personal Goals

Dreams are not Goals

Before we move on, we need to briefly mention an important distinction between dreams and goals. "Follow your dream" is a piece of advice you may have heard, and it feels correct but, in truth, it's neither helpful nor generally achievable. Dreams are vague aspirations. We hear stories about people who have followed a dream to create a successful business or found success in some other realm. The problem is, we only ever hear from the people who succeed, not from the far larger number who end up penniless and disillusioned because they pursue a hopeless dream.

Dreams are valuable. They provide passion, commitment, and hope. If you confuse dreams with goals, you are probably headed for disaster. How can you tell the difference? Goals are SMART. That is, if you test them for being specific, measurable, achievable, relevant, and timed, you can come up with clear and defined answers. Dreams aren't SMART, and you cannot define a clear path to achieving them. Don't abandon your dreams, but don't confuse them with the goals that will give you focus and commitment every single day.

Killing Self-Pity

Self-pity, feeling sorry for yourself, and feeling that all the problems you face aren't your fault, are prime enemies of mental toughness. If you are going to become mentally tough, you must banish self-pity.

Mentally tough people are in control of their lives. They know both their strengths and their weaknesses, and they use this knowledge to achieve their goals. If they fail, they accept responsibility, learn from the process, and move on. People suffering from self-pity blame other people, circumstances, or the world in general when things go wrong. They see their place in life as passive, and they often complain vehemently about that situation. Think about people you know who spend a great deal of time complaining. Are they people who are successful? Generally, the answer is no. People who surrender to self-pity are much more likely to give up when faced with challenges simply because they don't see that they have the ability to change things. Complainers generally lack mental toughness, and successful people generally do not complain even when they face adversity.

Self-pity is a choice you make, not something you are born with. It's a way of thinking that can become deeply embedded in your personality and can undermine everything you do. If you catch yourself complaining, stop. Complaining doesn't change anything. It simply reinforces your view that you are dealing with forces outside your control and tells others that you have a passive attitude.

If you are unhappy about something, think instead of what you can do to change the situation. Take steps to make those things happen. If someone's attitude or behavior is causing problems, tell them, in a way that won't leave them feeling resentful and angry. If circumstances are preventing you from achieving something, think about how you can effect changes to make things better. If that isn't possible, try reframing the problem. Can you change what you are trying to achieve into something that is possible?

Most of all, be an active achiever, not a complainer. If you do feel a sudden twinge of self-pity when things go wrong, there is an antidote called gratitude. Most of us, and particularly those of us who live in the developed world, have a great deal to be thankful for. These are often circumstances we take for granted or don't think about at all. Take a moment to consider what makes you feel grateful.

<u>Exercise 10: Things to be grateful for</u>

Willpower and Self-Discipline

You're going to need both willpower and self-discipline to develop the habit of mental toughness. It's worth taking a moment to discuss just what we mean by those terms because, although they are often used synonymously, they are distinctly different.

Willpower is the ability to defer satisfying short-term temptations in order to meet long-term goals. When you don't eat a sugary snack because you're on a diet, that's willpower. Willpower is important, and it's something that many of us feel that we lack. Respondents to the annual *Stress in America Survey* (carried out by the *American Psychological Association*) regularly cite lack of willpower as the main reason they are not able to persist in positive life changes. Many people believe that willpower is a finite resource, like fuel in the tank of a car. As each day progresses, you use up your store of willpower, and it gets harder and harder to resist temptation.

Self-discipline is similar, but it isn't about resisting temptation. Rather, it's about making decisions that directly support the achievement of a long-term goal. A common misperception is that self-discipline is something unpleasant or even obsessive, but that isn't the case. It is about taking control and making decisions that support your long-term goals. Willpower may decline each day but self-discipline is always there to replace it. When you have both willpower and self-discipline, you will always be able to find the ability to continue no matter what happens.

Neither willpower nor self-discipline are inherent. Both can be developed and strengthened through repetition. Both are closely linked to having long-term goals. You can't make decisions that support your long-term future unless you know what you want that future to look like. Both are also closely associated with the ability to delay gratification, the ability to reject an immediate temptation in order to make progress towards a long-term goal. What can you do to boost your willpower and self-discipline? Here are four proven strategies:

> **Remove distractions and temptations.** It is easier to resist temptations when you remove them from your immediate environment. If you have an issue with junk food, for example, get rid of all the junk food in your fridge and keep your work area clear of snacks. If you are tempted to spend your evenings and weekends slumped in front of the television rather than doing something productive, don't automatically switch on the TV as soon as you come into the house. Find a place to work where you can't see the set. Make watching television a reward, something you do after you have completed a task.

> **Make a plan.** Think about how you can develop your willpower and self-discipline. For example, stress and fatigue can lead you to make instinct-

driven decisions based on satisfying short-term gratification. Exercise reduces stress and makes you less prone to fatigue. Make a plan that includes exercise in your daily routine. Eat regular, small, healthy meals. Blood sugar levels that are too low or too high can reduce both willpower and self-discipline.

Don't try to do too much, too quickly. You cannot turn laziness into absolute commitment overnight. Willpower and self-discipline can become habits (and we'll talk more about forming positive habits a little later), but these new habits take time to form. Instead, plan to take small, consistent steps over a period of weeks or months. Celebrate progress and learn to recognize that willpower and self-discipline aren't nasty things that you have to put up with. They are signs that you are truly in control of your life.

Learn to focus. If you can give 100% of your attention to what you are doing right now, not only will you perform better, but you are much less likely to be distracted or to give in to temptation. How do you learn to focus? By doing it! Block your day into segments where you deal with a single issue. Focus on that issue and nothing else until it's resolved. Don't take breaks except between segments, and schedule breaks to allow time for eating and exercise. Taking time out of your busy schedule for a work-out, a brisk walk, or a healthy snack isn't time wasted. Exercise and healthy eating improve your ability to focus and boost willpower and self-discipline.

Embracing boredom is the key to mastery

Mastering any activity involves boredom. Whether you want to learn to play a musical instrument, paint, write, take part in a new a sport, or just to get better at what you already do, you need to spend time practicing. You must repeat that activity over and over until you can do it without thought. To many people, the thought of doing the same thing repeatedly seems boring and they find that off-putting. But mental toughness requires making friends with repetition and learning not to avoid it but to embrace it.

Begin by accepting that doing anything well requires endless repetition. No matter how naturally talented you may be or what innate abilities you have, this idea is true. It even applies to creative activities that we think of as spontaneous, like writing and painting. The author whose books you love didn't just get up one morning and say, "Hey, I think I'll write a book." They spent years perfecting their craft, writing day after day until they were able to write in a way that is engaging and entertaining. Take the example of the artist Pablo Picasso. Looking at his cubist and surrealist paintings, you might think they were done in a sudden burst of inspiration and with little prior thought. However, before he ever thought about painting in such a novel way, Picasso spent 17 years learning the techniques of conventional painting. Only when he had absolute mastery of these skills did he move on to paintings that look as though they were created spontaneously.

No matter what innate talents you have, mastering a new skill requires time and repetition.

You must master elements of whatever craft you practice. Mastery probably won't involve great creativity, but even if we are talking about the skills of using spreadsheets or accountancy software, it's essential that you have it. Why? Because mastery is a basic prerequisite for the confidence you need to trust your own skills and abilities. Without that confidence, you will never achieve mental toughness.

How do you get comfortable with boredom? The first step is acknowledging that you're bored. Our brains like to be stimulated by new things and, if faced with a familiar task, we may find our minds drifting. We may try to find excuses not to do that activity. These responses to familiar tasks are normal but, once you recognize that you're bored (or trying to avoid that feeling) you can begin to deal with the emotions it brings.

Having the personal goals we discussed earlier helps a great deal in dealing with boredom. If you have your equivalent of a toy Porsche on your desk, that reminds you why you're doing what you are doing and it provides the motivation to continue. You can also remind yourself that every repetition of a mundane task takes you closer to mastery.

There are also simple strategies to make repeated tasks a little easier. Time yourself on those tasks, and turn them into a game to try to beat your own record. Give yourself a small reward if you succeed. Try to schedule your day by alternating familiar tasks with new ones. Try meditation. You don't have to leave your desk and adopt a lotus position on the floor. Studies have shown that taking even two minutes to do nothing but sit back and focus completely on your breathing can reduce stress and increase concentration.

Remind yourself that, unlikely though it sounds, boredom can actually boost creativity. A 2014 study carried out by the University of Central Lancashire[9] took two groups of test subjects. One group was given a stimulating task, writing about something new. The other group were given a boring task. They were asked to copy numbers out of a telephone book. Immediately afterwards, both groups were asked to complete a task that required creativity and original thought. The group that had been engaged in the boring task beforehand consistently did better. That's why interspersing boring tasks with those that requires creativity may work so well.

Enduring boredom is temporary. Success is not.

You'll notice that we have not discussed being bored because you have nothing to do. The reason is simple: If you have clear goals backed-up by willpower and self-discipline, you will <u>never</u> have nothing to do. There is always something you can do to move closer to your goals. Read about how other people have succeeded, learn new

---

[9] *Does Being Bored Make Us More Creative?* Mann, Sandi and Cadman, Rebekah, University of Central Lancashire, Creativity Research Journal, 2014.

skills or simply do chores around the house to overcome laziness and bolster willpower and self-discipline.

Exercise 12: Boredom

Is this the right time to quit?

We have already spoken about dealing with failure and the value of persistence, but we also need to talk about knowing when to quit. Mentally tough people know how to keep going through adversity, but they also know the right time to quit. This strategy is known as smart quitting and it is an important attribute of the most successful people. In 2008, two American psychologists, Heather Lench and Linda Levine, conducted a fascinating experiment[10] on the value of quitting. Subjects were asked to complete a number of anagrams. The test was timed and participants were told to complete the anagrams in order. However, the first anagram was unsolvable. The only people who scored well were those who gave up on the first anagram and continued with the rest. Subjects with positive goals aimed at attaining success scored consistently well. Those with negative goals aimed at avoiding failure often got stuck on the first anagram.

Having positive goals is an important context for quitting, but you also need to be sure you are quitting for the right reasons. Quitting because you're tired or because continuing seems difficult is never a good idea. Quitting because of an emotional response to setbacks or because

---

[10] *Goals and responses to failure: Knowing when to hold them and when to fold them,* by Heather C. Lench and Linda J. Levine, Motivation and Emotion, 2008.

you're concerned about what others will think are also not helpful. Conversely, not quitting because you are afraid of failure or what people will think or because you have already invested so much time and effort in something (the "sunk-cost fallacy") aren't helpful, either.

Instead, you need to take an objective look at progress or lack of it. You need to think about how your current efforts are contributing towards attaining your goals. You must consider whether your time and effort might be better spent in another area. Most of all, you have to see that quitting does not equate to failure as long as you learn from the experience. Persistence is important, but real mental toughness means recognizing the moment when refocusing your energy on something different is the best way forward.

<u>Exercise 13: Knowing when to quit</u>

Making your inner voice positive

We all have an inner voice that provides a constant commentary on our lives. We get so used to this voice that we no longer hear it. Sometimes, it takes a conscious effort to hear what the inner voice is saying. Some people find meditation a good way to learn to hear that inner voice. If we can listen to what it's saying, very often that voice is critical and negative, undermining our confidence and mocking our efforts to change. No matter how hard we try, the voice may be telling us that we'll never succeed, that we're just not good enough. Where does it come from? No one is certain, though most experts think it originates during childhood. Everyone has this inner voice, even the most confident and mentally tough people. It becomes a problem if you allow it to control your behavior. This inner voice can be the opposite of mental toughness, but the good news is that you can learn to be more conscious of it and to recognize what it says as spurious and unhelpful.

The first step towards reducing the impact of your inner critic is to actually listen to what it's saying. While we are striving to improve, the inner voice may be whispering that we will never succeed. When we're trying to succeed at something new, it may be telling us that we always fail. That inner voice can be useful, helping to regulate our behavior and not repeat past mistakes. But it often becomes stuck in negative patterns that can undermine everything we do. If you catch your inner voice telling you something negative, stop for a moment to objectively scrutinize what it's telling you.

Failure is often a focal point for the inner critic. It loves to bring up past failures and to use these as evidence that you are likely to fail again. But, as we have discussed, failure is not something to be afraid of. If you listen to that inner voice, you will never try anything that involves a risk of failure, which essentially means never trying anything at all. If you learn to see failure as an opportunity and a step towards eventual success, that step will minimize the effect of your inner voice. Many things that your inner critic will say can be countered in this way, by looking at them objectively and weighing the evidence. To succeed, your inner critic depends on an emotional response to what it says. If you can use logic and analysis to lessen such a response, you reduce the negative impact of the voice.

It's also important to look at the people you spend time with and consider the effect they have on your state of mind. Some people are so relentlessly negative and pessimistic that they sound a lot like that inner critic brought to life. In fact, your inner critic will seize on what these people say, telling you "Look – I was right!" Do you know anyone like that? If so, you may want to spend less time with them. Their pessimism can be infectious! Instead, look for people who share your optimism ad positive outlook.

Thinking about other people can be another good way of dealing with your inner critic. Imagine if a friend were to come to you and explain how a negative inner voice was making them doubt their abilities and abandon their plans. What would you advise? You'd probably try to understand just what it was that the inner critic was undermining, and then use logic to point out that person's good points and how they could use those to overcome potential problems. Part of the issue is that it's just much easier for us to see the obvious in other people than ourselves, and most of us find it easier to be compassionate to other people than ourselves.

Another strategy for dealing with a negative inner critic is to use a psychological approach known as the "wise advocate." This approach involves visualizing a person. It can be a family member, a friend, someone you know (or have known) or even a historical figure whose accomplishments you admire. Who they are is not important. This visualized person must be wise, compassionate, kind, supportive, and they must truly care and want the best for you. It must also be a person whose views and advice you respect. Imagine describing a situation to this person. How would they respond and what would they advise you to do? The guidance from this wise advocate will always be positive and in your best interests. Visualizing what they would advise can be a powerful antidote to negative messages from your inner critic.

That inner voice does fulfill a useful purpose: it helps to avoid compulsive behavior by making us question what we plan to do and think about whether that really is a good idea. It becomes a problem for many people when it becomes relentlessly pessimistic and unsupportive, undermining our confidence and willingness to try new things. You must learn to listen to what that inner voice is saying. By doing that you can begin to recognize when it's giving you bad advice. Using the advice of your wise advocate will help to lessen its impact.

<u>Exercise 14: Hearing and directing your inner critic</u>

Establishing the habit of mental toughness

Habits are powerful drivers of human behavior. Habits account for far more of what we do every single day than most of us realize. But what are habits? Generally, these are behaviors that we do without conscious thought or planning. They can be helpful because we don't have to give thought to often-repeated tasks. Take your morning drive to work, for example. You get from your home to your place of work and, for most people, during that journey they don't think once about how much to turn the steering wheel or when to press the accelerator. These are habitual actions that we no longer have to think about, leaving our minds free to focus on signals, other traffic, and pedestrians.

However, habits can also be destructive and unhelpful. If we learn to deal with stress through alcohol, that is entirely unhelpful. Any stressful situation can leave us craving a drink, even when drinking is completely inappropriate. If we let a fear of failure become a habit that blocks us from attainment, that is also unhelpful. Before we talk about how to form positive habits, we first need to understand a little of the psychology and physiology of habits.

In psychology, there is something known as Hebb's Law, which states that when brain nerve cells are activated in the same pattern repeatedly, they eventually form a fixed neural circuit. The more this circuit is used, the stronger it becomes. An analogy is to consider walking across a rough piece of ground. Initially, you might choose any route but, over time, a path becomes worn in the undergrowth. When you subsequently travel in this area, you are far more likely to retrace your steps over the emerging pathway.

Likewise, when we learn to use alcohol in response to stress, this response eventually becomes a fixed neural circuit in our brain, a habit. If we feel stressed, our brain tells us that a drink is the answer. If we fear failure, our brain tells us that the answer is to avoid anything that carries a risk of failure. Happily, these circuits are not permanently fixed, something that was previously believed. Instead, new neural circuits can be formed and old ones discarded. The ability of our brains to form new neural circuits has been proven through stroke victims who have been able to reassign even fundamental behaviors like walking to new parts of the brain.

Psychologists call this ability of the brain to re-form neural circuits "plasticity." Treatment of conditions like alcohol and substance abuse and compulsive behaviors has led to another discovery: "self-directed neuroplasticity". That sounds complicated, but actually, it isn't. It simply means that if you make a conscious effort to adopt a new behavior, it eventually becomes embedded in new neural circuits. In other words, it becomes a habit.

Think about that for a moment because it is both incredibly powerful and liberating. If you can identify a new behavior that you want to become automatic, all you have to do is keep it up until a new neural circuit is formed, and it will become a habit. How long will that take? There is no definite answer. It seems to depend on the individual and the behavior. Most estimates suggest somewhere between 30 and 90 days. What is certain is that if you are able to keep up a new and positive behavior long enough, that process will actually change your brain.

There are several methods of retraining your brain, but one of the most popular is the four-step approach developed by Dr. Jeffrey M. Schwartz[11].

- Step 1 is learning to listen to your inner voice and, in particular, to what Dr Schwartz calls "deceptive brain messages." These are the messages from

---

[11] *You Are Not Your Brain: The 4-Step Solution for Changing Bad Habits, Ending Unhealthy Thinking, and Taking Control of Your Life* by Jeffrey M. Schwartz M.D. and Rebecca Gladding M.D., Avery, 2011.

- Step 2 is reframing. Learn to analyze these messages and see which are preventing you from achieving your goals.
- Step 3 is refocusing, or deliberately undertaking new and more positive behaviors. Even if you perform the new behavior while you are still troubled by your inner critic, you will begin to create the neural circuits that support the new behaviors.
- Step 4 is revaluing, continuing to objectively assess the messages coming from your inner critic and seeing those which are deceptive.

Let's look at a simple example. When you get home from work, you are tired and probably stressed. Your habit is to grab a beer and slump in front of the television, something that you do all evening. Every evening. Soon, reaching for a beer and the remote become habits embedded in neural circuits that are activated every time you walk in the door after work. What you'd like to do is to take some exercise in the evening by taking a walk, going to the gym, or going for a jog. But it all seems like too much effort and instead, you find yourself spending every evening on the couch before going to bed, irritated with yourself and a little disgusted by your inability to do something more productive.

The good news is that you can change that behavior. The bad news is that it's all up to you. You actually have to want to change, and that's where having clear goals helps. If you sit down and write what you want, that helps to clarify what you want to change. If one of those goals is to get fitter and perhaps lose a little weight, then that's good. Then, you actually have to make a conscious effort not to go to the fridge and turn on the television when you come home after work. You must make yourself go for a walk or a run or go to the gym. At first, it's going to be really tough because your existing neural circuits are telling you that it's all wrong, that instead you should be having a drink and watching soaps. Focusing on your goals helps you to find the motivation to begin the new behavior. That motivation is maintained by the knowledge that you are permanently rewiring your brain in a more positive way.

Soon, when you come home from work, you'll find yourself looking forward to that walk or jog. You'll automatically reach for your running shoes rather than heading for the fridge. And when you go to bed, you'll feel the satisfaction of knowing that you are making progress towards your goals and getting fitter. Getting rid of unwanted habits and adopting new and more positive habits is really that simple. It isn't easy, because you have to make yourself undertake the new activity even while your existing neural circuits are telling you to do something else. Overcoming those messages from your brain takes determination and commitment but you can do it and you can keep it up until the new behavior becomes a habit.

The elements of mental toughness described in this chapter can become habits, too. With clear goals to provide motivation, you can establish new behaviors that will enable you to:

- Kill self-pity
- Boost willpower and self-discipline
- Help deal with boredom
- Know when to quit and refocus
- Think positively

By adopting these behaviors, you can retrain your brain to accept the habits of mental toughness automatically and constantly. All you have to do is decide where to start.

Exercise 15: Identifying a behavior you want to change

Chapter 6: 10-Step Checklist for Mental Toughness

This final chapter provides a review of everything we have discussed in the form of 10 headings, each followed by questions. Read each section and answer the questions.

This is not a test. You will not be given a score at the end that will tell you whether or not you have achieved mental toughness. Instead, these review points are provided as a way to assess the progress you have made. You may want to come back to this section many times to reassess how far you have been able to develop your mental toughness. Read the questions and think about your answers. If you answer "No" to any question, think about what you need to do to change this answer to "Yes." Go back and read the relevant part of this book for guidance, and take the action required.

1. Take responsibility

The very first step towards developing mental toughness involves taking responsibility. There are two parts. The first is accepting that you have the ability to make a choice about developing your own mental toughness. This book explains just what mental toughness is and why it is important, but only you can choose to incorporate it in your life.

Have you made that choice, and are you committed to doing what is needed? If you are going to succeed, you really need to be able to answer "Yes!" without any reservations. If you can't, perhaps you need to revisit the personal goals you created in Exercise 9. These goals must be sufficiently important to you that you are willing to put in the effort required to achieve them.

The second part involves accepting that you have the ability to choose what you do and in particular, to choose how you respond to problems and setbacks. If you find yourself complaining about other people or circumstances, stop! If things don't go as planned, ask yourself what <u>you</u> could have done differently to change the outcome. Complaining achieves nothing. Staying focused on what you can do differently next time actually makes a difference. You can choose to see the world as a place in which you are powerless, or you can choose to actively change your life through mental toughness.

- Are you ready to commit to becoming mentally tough?
- Are you committed to becoming an active achiever, not a passive complainer?

2. Control your emotions

Emotions matter, and all of us are subject to these feelings. To become mentally tough, you must master those emotions. The first step towards that mastery is clearly understanding the emotions that affect you and seeing where they come from. Meditation can help. You don't have to meditate for long or adopt the lotus position. Just take five minutes somewhere you won't be disturbed or interrupted. Close your eyes and think about nothing except your breathing.

What do you feel? Most people feel refreshed and invigorated, but you should also become aware of your inner voice and the emotions it provokes. You will also be able to see how these feelings make you act. Positive emotions lead to positive behaviors. Joy and contentment lead to behavior driven by compassion and kindness. Jealously and guilt make you act unkindly towards others. However, simply becoming aware of negative emotions can lessen their affect.

Empathy is a key part of mental toughness and it allows us to understand other people's emotions. Without it, our personal and work relationships are much more difficult and less productive.

- Are you truly aware of the negative emotions that you experience?
- Can you see how these emotions make you act in negative ways?
- Do you have strategies to deal with these emotions?
- Do you understand the emotions that other people experience, and can you identify how these emotions make them act?

3. Think positive

Negative emotions can be banished by conscious effort. When you become aware that you are experiencing self-pity, anger, or worry, make the effort instead to think about the things you are grateful for. When you find yourself focused on failures and disappointments, make the effort instead to think about success and achievement.

The more you wallow in negative feelings, the more they will undermine your resolve and sap your energy.

Listen to your inner voice. What is it telling you? Is it critical and negative, focusing on perceived weaknesses, and telling you that you are going to fail? Or is it supportive, looking at past successes and telling you how to use your strengths to succeed? If it is negative, you can confront your inner voice with logic and objectivity. If you show that it is being unreasonably pessimistic you can train it instead to accentuate the positive.

- Overall, do you feel positive about yourself and your future?
- When you listen to your inner voice, is it supportive?
- Have you visualized a wise advocate?

4. Face up to your fears

Fear is natural and even helpful because it helps us to avoid potentially harmful situations. If unchecked, fear can dominate us and make us avoid change and challenge. Sometimes, it can be difficult to recognize when fear is holding us back from doing something that would help us to achieve our goals. We may tell ourselves that we are being prudent or cautious, but really, we are being blocked by fear.

Once recognized, fear can be lessened by using well-known techniques. These strategies involve exploring the roots of our fears and adopting strategies to lessen their impact.

- Can you think of an occasion when fear has stopped you from achieving something?
- Have you used the techniques of facing your fears and pre-mortem to lessen fear?

5. Get comfortable with risk

Making positive changes almost always involves some level of risk. We are not talking about the kind of risk associated with driving too fast or gambling recklessly, but the risk that something you try may fail. Facing that kind of risk is inevitable if you want to make positive changes to your life, but many people find any kind of risk to be a frightening prospect.

Your brain can be trained to accept risk. This process is called "desensitizing" and it does not mean that you have to skydive or begin a different dangerous hobby. Simply make the effort to try different things every day. Find a new route to work, eat something different for lunch, go for an evening drink with someone new, or learn a new skill or ability. By making these small changes, your brain gradually becomes used to being exposed to the risk of new experiences.

- Can you think of an example where avoiding risk has caused you not to do something?
- Have you tried a new activity recently to desensitize yourself to risk?

6. Deal effectively with failure

Associated with risk is failure. If you try anything new, there is a possibility that you may fail. Some people use that as an excuse not to try. Mental toughness means being willing to accept failure, to learn from it, and to move on.

The most significant and useful learning in life comes from failure. Failure can teach us where we went wrong, leading to an understanding of how to do it right next time. If you are open to learning, failure can help you make progress towards your goals. Never assume that failure is inevitable, and always aim for success. However, accept that no one is perfect and that you may fail along the way.

- Do you truly regard failure as an opportunity for learning?
- Can you think of a past failure that has led to success?

7. Persist

Achieving mastery is an essential prerequisite for success in any field. But mastery takes time and the ability to deal with boredom and repetition. Mental toughness means understanding that time is required to achieve mastery. Mental toughness also means being able to delay gratification, to put up with short-term inconvenience and repetitive effort in order to achieve long-term goals.

Persistence also means dealing effectively with failure, using it as a learning opportunity that will allow us to make progress towards our goals. We most often give up on something because we don't have a sufficiently powerful goal to keep us on track.

- Have you ever given up on something and regretted that later?
- Do your goals keep you going even when things are challenging?

8. But know when to quit…

Persistence is necessary, but it must be tempered with the realization that sometimes, quitting is the best option. Fear can make us keep going with something long after it is clear that activity is not leading us closer to our goals. You only have so much time, and you must constantly review what you are doing and what your work is achieving. If something is not productive, stop, learn, and move on.

Quitting must be a conscious decision. You are in charge of quitting just as you are of every other aspect of your life. Don't just let things drift. Be in control, and decide when to keep going and when to quit. Never quit just because continuing is difficult or tiring. Quit because continuing is not helping you progress towards your goals.

- Have you ever kept going with something even though that was not productive?
- If you are thinking about quitting, have you examined your reasons?

9. Think like a Royal Marine

Royal Marine training emphasizes four qualities that add up to mental toughness. These are unity, humility, adaptability and fortitude. Adaptability is about seeing opportunity in uncertainty, being willing to take risks, and benefiting from the learning that comes from failure. Fortitude is about persistence, keeping going when you are tired, discouraged, or demotivated.

The other two qualities are equally important, but they are frequently neglected as elements of mental toughness. Unity is about being unselfish, being team-oriented, empathetic and supportive. Humility means accepting that there are always things that you can learn and always areas in which you can improve.

Being mentally tough means that you have <u>all four</u> qualities.

- Do you have unity, humility, adaptability, and fortitude?

10. Take action

"Inaction breeds doubt and fear. Action breeds confidence and courage. If you want to conquer fear, do not sit home and think about it. Go out and get busy."

Dale Carnegie

You will never succeed only by thinking about what you might change. Success only comes from action. You now know what to do to develop the mental toughness you need to succeed. Now, you must do it. To make that possible, you require plans.

The goals you identified in Exercise 9 are essential. They are the objectives that you are working towards, and they help to bolster willpower and self-discipline in difficult times. But you also need short-term plans that help you progress towards those long-term goals. You may have your own method of creating plans, but how to you answer the following questions?

- Have you made a plan for the next three months? This plan should include objectives you want to accomplish that support your long-term goals. These objectives may include learning new skills, practicing new abilities such as unity, humility, and empathy, and applying positive thinking. At the end of the three-month period, review progress and make a new plan for the following three months. Decide what you will keep working on and what you are going to quit. If you have experienced any failures, think about how you learned from these setbacks and what you will do to avoid the same failures in the future.

- Have you made a plan for the next month? This monthly plan should identify at least one behavior you want to change using self-directed neuroplasticity. It really does not matter what behavior you choose. It can be something as simple as making your bed first thing every morning or getting in to work 15 minutes early. The important thing is acknowledging that you can change your behavior and that, if you maintain the new positive behavior, that behavior will become a habit. Try to target at least one new positive behavior every month. Review at the end of each month, and assess whether you successfully changed. Once you are confident with this approach, you can begin to use it to target new behaviors. These may be intended to desensitize you to taking risks, face your fears, build your willpower and self-discipline, think positively, and to persist.

- Do you make a "to-do" list every day? When you are trying to build mental toughness at the same time as spending time working, having relationships, and finding time for hobbies and exercise, it is all too easy to feel overwhelmed. A good way to ensure you use your time effectively is to make a list, first thing, of the tasks you want to complete that day. You can write the list on paper or by using an app. Include tasks for building mental toughness such as desensitizing yourself to risk by trying new experiences.

- Do you review progress, every day? At the end of each day, think what you have achieved, particularly in terms of making progress towards your goals and adopting the habits of mental toughness. Think about how a new behavior has allowed you to respond more effectively to a situation at work or in your personal life. Celebrate success and achieving important milestones. If you complete a particular task or achieve a new skill, treat yourself.

Exercises

Exercise 1: The enemies of mental toughness

In Chapter 2, we looked at seven states of mind that inhibit mental toughness. These were:

- Self-pity

- Self-doubt

- Laziness

- Perfectionism

- Fear

- Negative emotions

- Self-limiting beliefs

Take five minutes to work through the list, and highlight those that have affected you. Be honest. Overcoming these states of mind are some of the most important challenges you will have to overcome on your journey to mental toughness. It is important that you identify those challenges you need to work on.

Try to identify those states of mind that have become habitual responses. Do you always get angry when things don't go your way? Or do you feel sorry for yourself? Now, write down the states that have the most impact on your life. Don't worry, you won't be sharing these notes with anyone else. You may want to come back to this exercise later to see if you have improved.

Exercise 2: Negative Emotions

This exercise will take a little longer, but it is important that you recognize and identify the emotions you feel.

First, think about how you respond when things go wrong. In particular, think about what emotions you experience. Does failure make you angry? Anxious? Afraid? Guilty? Sad? Write down the emotions you feel. There will probably be more than one, so take the time to think carefully and make sure you identify all the emotions.

Now, next to each emotion, write down how that emotion made you act. Perhaps anger made you behave unpleasantly towards a colleague of friend? Maybe embarrassment made you vow never to put yourself in the same situation again? Did jealousy make you act nastily towards someone else? There aren't any right answers here. Everyone responds differently and some of the things you are describing may make you cringe, but you do need to develop the skills not just to understand how you feel but to think about how that makes you act.

Now, write down how you are going to avoid acting the same way in the future. If anger is an issue that causes you to lash out, think about strategies for changing that. Take a deep breath, count to 10, whatever works for you. If embarrassment is the issue, what can you do to reduce this emotion in the future?

It is beyond the scope of this book to give you strategies for dealing with every emotion. Instead, this exercise is about beginning to think about negative emotions. If you can do that objectively, you'll find that you respond differently next time you feel that emotion.

Exercise 3: Empathy

Think about the last occasion during which a friend, colleague, or partner was unhappy. Do you really understand what was causing their unhappiness? Can you identify the emotions they were experiencing and see what caused those feelings? Now, think about the answers to these questions:

- In the same circumstances, what emotions would you have felt? Would they have been the same? If not, why not?

- How would those emotions have caused you to respond? Would have acted differently? Why?

- Would your response have been reasonable and effective? Would there have been better ways to respond?

- Think of someone you admire (it doesn't matter if you actually know the person or even if they're real). How would they have responded in the same situation? Would that have been a better way to respond? How can you act in ways that are closer to those of that person you admire?

Take the time to think about how much empathy you have. Are you confident that you understand the emotions the other person was feeling? Are you able to put yourself in their shoes and think through their actions without being judgmental? In short, are you empathetic? If not, increasing your empathy is something you may want to work on.

For more detail you can try taking an EQ test. You will find lots of these tests on-line. Try to use one from a reputable organization, such as those provided by *Psychology Today* or the *Institute for Health and Human Potential,* and think about what the results tell you.

Exercise 4: Dealing with failure

Take the time to write down details of five recent failures in your life. They can big or small, anything from failing to sink a three-foot putt to failing to win a major contract.

Now, the tricky bit: Describe how you responded to those failures. Write down whether those failures prompted a tantrum, denial, guilt, or self-doubt. Think about what your emotions were and how they caused you to act. Be completely honest and include as much detail as possible.

How could you have acted differently and more constructively? For each failure, write down at least one idea for how you could have responded in a more positive way. What did you learn from each failure?

Hopefully you can see that relatively small changes in the behavior that results from failure can provide a much more positive way forward.

Exercise 5: Naming your fear

When you are afraid, it is difficult to be objective, but that's just what you need to do when naming your fears. Think of an activity that you are putting off or that you just can't seem to get started on. Now, undertake these two short writing tasks:

- Write an account of the activity that describes what it is you need to do and why you are avoiding it. Write it as if it will be read by someone who doesn't know you or anything about the task.

- Now, write a short, persuasive piece that argues against doing this task. Be as descriptive as you can. Include the positive points but try to persuade the reader that undertaking this task is a bad idea.

How do you feel about that task now? Nameless fears, fears of the unknown, are the most destructive and insistent. Just taking the time to look objectively at what it is you fear can actually make it lessen.

Exercise 6: What's the worst that can happen?

This technique involves applying a bit of imagination, and it can even be fun in a macabre kind of way.

Think about some new idea or different course of action you are considering.

Take some time to think about the very worst position you might find yourself in if you follow this new idea. Don't hold back. Be as dramatic and over-the-top as you want. Visualize yourself living in a cardboard box under a bridge, abandoned by your partner after your house and car have been repossessed. And it's snowing.

- How did you get there?

- Specifically, what were the decisions and choices you made that led to that situation? Write your answer down.

- How could you have made different decisions that would have avoided that worst-case scenario? Write your answers down.

Facing your fears by imagining the very worst that can happen has been helping people to overcome fear since Seneca the Younger first introduced the idea 2,000 years ago. It can help you, too.

Exercise 7: Take a humility test

How do you know if you have humility? Read the following statements and think about a recent situation you have been involved with, either successful or not. It can from your work or your personal life but it should be something that led to discussion afterwards about what happened.

I made a mess of that. It's my fault. Sorry.

- Tell me where I went wrong.

- I'm not sure what to do and I need some help.

- How can I help?

- I know that I have things to learn and room to improve.

- You did well.

- I can't take the credit for that.

- I'm listening...

Can you imagine making any of these statements as part of the after-event discussion? Out loud and in front of other people? Really? Be honest because many of us struggle with giving praise, admitting that we have failed, or that we need help.

If you can imagine making these statements, and even better if you regularly do, then congratulations, you already have humility. If on the other hand, you really cannot imagine making these statements, you may have a problem. Perhaps your ego is getting in the way. If you cannot see any reason to make these statements because you never make mistakes, don't have anything to learn, and never need help, then you lack humility.

To increase your humility, you may want to make a conscious effort to use these statements (or similar ones) next time you are involved in discussing a success or failure.

Exercise 8: What did you learn today?

Take a few moments at the end of the day to write down what you learned that day. It doesn't have to be anything big. Did you learn a new word or phrase, did you learn something new about a topic that interests you, did you find a new route to work, did you learn something new about a colleague or partner?

On virtually any day, you will learn something new. Generally, you will not even notice that you are learning unless you stop and think carefully about the new knowledge. Thinking about what you are learning reinforces two important facts about you: that you acquire new experience and knowledge every day and that you always have the capacity to learn and improve. These are essential attributes of humility.

Exercise 9: Setting Personal Goals

Exercise 9 is a complex exercise, so don't rush it.

Begin by thinking about what you want to achieve over the next 10 years. This objective can be broad and fairly vague. It is just the starting point. Be honest here. You aren't going to be sharing your goals with anyone. Writing ideas out is a great way of clarifying your thinking. Don't feel pressured to say that you want to help people and make the world a better place. These goals must matter to you. If you really feel passionate about philanthropy or altruism, that's great. But if your goal is something more selfish like owning a sports car, buying a place on the beach, or retiring in financial security, that's OK too. These goals must be relevant and motivational for you, not to anybody else.

Then you need to identify the SMART goals that you need in order to achieve your 10-year objective. You may want to break these goals down even further into objectives that you can reach in the next month or two and those that will take longer. Some goals may even be sequential and dependent. You may want to seek a promotion at work, but you might need an additional qualification first, for example.

Take the time to write down these goals. Give detail for each. Be clear about what you want to achieve, how you're going to do it, and when you aim to have it complete.

This list of goals will become both your road map to the future and your motivation. Building mental toughness will take time and sustained effort. Your desire to reach these goals is what will drive you onwards. Are they important enough that you are willing to devote time and effort to achieving them? If not, you may want to revise this list several times until you identify your life goal.

Setting these goals will also help you to develop the skill of delaying gratification. If you know you are working towards defined and clear long-term objectives, it is much easier to resist temptation and avoid laziness.

Once you have finished, keep this list somewhere safe. You will be coming back to it in the future. At least every three months, or more often if you feel the need, review your list of goals. Are they all still relevant and motivational? If not, consider changing existing goals or adding new goals. During the review, note against each goal the progress you have made towards it.

Exercise 10: Things to be grateful for

Write down five things for which you are thankful. Be creative. Be thankful for good health, good weather, for having a job that allows you to support your family, for having a loving partner, for living in a place that is not blighted by war or famine. In everyone's life, there are many things to be thankful for. Devoting time to gratitude is a powerful way to banish feelings of self-pity.

Exercise 11: Self-discipline

Write down five things that you find it difficult to do every day. These challenges can be anything from getting out of bed in good time, to washing up after you eat, to keeping your home tidy. We all have things we'd rather not do, but we become so used to not doing them or putting them off that we are barely aware of them anymore. That's why we are surprised when we end up with a sink stacked with dirty dishes and an apartment that looks as though a cyclone has swept through it.

Now, make another list of five things that you probably shouldn't be doing but you find difficult to resist. You may include anything from having a sugary snack with your morning coffee, to spending the evening propped in front of the television, or having an after-work drink every night.

Now, take a look at these lists, and pick one item from each. From now on, the task that you find difficult to do, you will do promptly, every day. You will make a conscious effort to resist temptation.

After resisting temptation and doing a task you normally avoid for one month, how does that make you feel? Doesn't it make you feel that you have the ability to take charge, to be in control of your own destiny? Doesn't that feel good? Now imagine extending that feeling into other parts of your life.

The good news is that by taking these small steps, you are building your willpower and self-discipline and, as you will learn, you are actually rewiring your brain. If you take it one step at a time, you can change your life in order to reach those long-term goals.

Exercise 12: Boredom

Write down five negative emotions you associate with boredom. Take the time to really think about these feelings, but you may include things like:

- Frustration

- Restlessness

- Pessimism

- Anger

- Anxiety

Think about a specific activity that causes you boredom. Consider the positive benefits that activity brings and the potential negative effects of not doing it. You will be able to see why the short-term emotions caused by boredom are worth enduring for the long-term benefits of the activity. You should be able to do this for any activity you find boring.

Exercise 13: Knowing when to quit

Think about three times in your personal experience when you quit something that you shouldn't have. Think about what it would have taken on your part to continue instead.

Now, think about three times in your personal experience when you have continued something beyond when it was productive or helpful, times when it would have been better to quit. What was it that kept you going when you should have stopped?

This exercise isn't about dwelling on past mistakes: it's about recognizing that there is no hard and fast rule about when is a good time to quit something. Learn to objectively assess benefit versus effort and focus your energy where it will bring the most benefit.

Exercise 14: Hearing and directing your inner critic

For one week, jot down examples of negative talk from your inner critic. Hearing that voice clearly won't be easy. You really have to listen carefully. If you feel apprehensive, unconfident, or just reluctant to do something, it may be because your inner voice has been suggesting problems and potential failure. It doesn't matter if the issues are big, small, or simply irritating. Try to get a list of at least 10 examples of when your inner voice has attempted to block you or undermine you.

At the end of the week, or when you have discovered 10 examples, stop and read them. Was there any truth in what your inner voice was saying? Often there isn't. The things that this voice tells you are intended to provoke an emotional response, and they often don't stand up to logical scrutiny. When your inner voice tells you "You always fail," for example, that is often not true. If you take the time to think about it, you can come up with lots of examples of where you haven't failed, despite what your inner voice suggested. Use the technique of imagining a friend is talking to you rather than your inner voice, and imagine how you'd respond.

You should be able to see that what your inner critic is saying is often neither true nor helpful. Each time you reject a negative message from your inner critic, the potential damage to your self-esteem and confidence is avoided. If you can continue to recognize and reject these negative messages then, over time, your inner voice will change, and you will find it becoming more supportive and helpful.

Exercise 15: Identifying a behavior you want to change

This exercise is similar to Exercise 11, but it's different in that you will actually be confirming your ability to rewire your own brain. Sit down and think about some aspect of your behavior that you would like to change to boost your mental toughness. It doesn't have to be massive. Perhaps you'd like to keep your home tidy or make your bed when you get up in the morning. Maybe you would like not to leave dirty dishes in the sink, or to get up a little earlier so you don't end up rushing in to work, or not to eat a bag of potato chips with lunch every day.

Now, think about what you need to do to change that behavior. In most cases, that's pretty obvious. You know what you should be doing. The problem is generally just not finding the willingness to do it. Make a commitment to yourself to undertake the new behavior and to keep it up for at least one month.

That's is all you have to do. Changing behavior is really as easy as making yourself do something new until it becomes a habit. It sounds overly simple, but it really works and is underpinned by relatively recent developments in psychology and neurobiology. You really can retrain your brain to work in the way that you want. If you see this approach working on one aspect of your life, you will gain the confidence to extend it into everything else you do.

Conclusion

Mental toughness is an often used, but little understood, term. Many people think it means being selfish, emotionless, or even fearless. In truth, it means none of these things, as you now clearly understand. Mental toughness is not a single ability but rather an approach that can carry you through the very worst surprises that life might give you. It also helps you at work, in relationships, and even in hobbies. Mental toughness is a prerequisite for success in any field.

However, mental toughness is complex, and there is no simple checklist you can use to assess whether you are mentally tough. The most important elements are:

- **Setting achievable goals.** You need motivation to sustain your willpower and self-discipline. This motivation comes from having clear goals that you are working towards. These must be goals that matter deeply to you and that will sustain you even when things get tough.
- **Taking control.** Being in control begins with recognizing that there are things you can change and things you cannot and focusing your time and energy on the latter. It means understanding that you have a choice in giving in to emotions like self-pity and negativity. It means understanding you can choose to be active and change the things you are not happy with, or you can be a passive complainer. One choice will change your life. The other will leave you disappointed and bitter.

- **Overcoming negative emotions.** There are times when everyone experiences anger, disappointment, frustration, jealousy, or even despair. Mental toughness means not allowing these negative emotions to dominate. It means making a conscious effort to increase the influence of positive emotions like compassion, hope, and joy. It means remaining optimistic despite setbacks and learning from the past but not being controlled by it. You cannot be mentally tough without learning positive thinking.
- **Knowing that mastery takes time.** If you want to become skilled at anything, you have to repeat it until you become proficient. There is no shortcut and repetition usually involves boredom. You must become comfortable with that fact and accept that short-term inconvenience and irritation are inevitable experiences on the road to long-term success.
- **Being willing to take risks.** If you want to make sure you never fail, there is only one certain way: never try. Mental toughness means being willing to risk failure because you recognize that is necessary to move closer to success.
- **Dealing effectively with setbacks.** Overcoming setbacks entails learning to deal with fear and problems. It also involves seeing learning opportunities even in failure. It also requires being resilient and persistent while accepting that there may come a time when quitting is the best option.
- **Being unselfish.** Mental toughness means knowing what you want and working towards that goal.

That dedication is not the same as being selfish. Working to support and advance other people is always important. The most successful people emerge from the most successful teams.

- **Remaining humble.** No matter how much you achieve, never denigrate another person, and never stop believing that there is room for improvement. Arrogance has no place in mental toughness, and it leads to a lack of progress.

If you look at virtually any successful person in any field, you will see all these qualities. The good news is that all these abilities are not innate. They can be learned and developed.

Unfortunately, mental toughness will not guarantee success in everything you do. However, a lack of mental toughness will guarantee that you do not succeed. If you truly want to change your life, adopting mental toughness is a great place to begin.

If you are not happy with your life right now, you really have only two choices. Either you can wait for luck to bring change, or you can develop mental toughness to understand what you want and develop the abilities you need to get it. Only one of these approaches will bring guaranteed improvement into your life.

Which do you choose?

YOUR FREE GIFT

We would like to give you a gift to thank you for purchasing this book. You can choose from any of our other published titles.

You can get immediate access to any of our books by clicking on the link below and joining our mailing list:

https://campsite.bio/mastertoday

YOU WILL
BE OKAY

YOU HAVE
NO CHOICE

www.ingramcontent.com/pod-product-compliance
Lightning Source LLC
LaVergne TN
LVHW011023200726

843509LV00011B/1181